Curries and Oriental Cookery

JOSCELINE DIMBLEBY

A SAINSBURY COOKBOOK

Published by Woodhead-Faulkner Limited
8 Market Passage, Cambridge CB2 3PF
for J Sainsbury Limited
Stamford House, Stamford Street, London SE1 9LL

First published 1980

Design: Ken Vail Graphic Design
Colour photography and cover picture: John Lee

Typesetting: Bedford Typesetters Limited
Printed and bound in Great Britain by
Hazell Watson & Viney Limited, Aylesbury, Bucks

Contents

Introduction

The English appetite is becoming more adventurous. In the past people have been known to comment that foreign food had "too much flavour". Nowadays we go abroad more for our holidays, and restaurants serving food from almost every country have sprung up not only in London but in most provincial towns. However, an outing to even a modest restaurant is every day more expensive and there are many delicious exotic dishes which, for some reason, never appear on the restaurant menu. It is far better to experiment at home.

This book is a practical introduction to exotic foods from India, China, the Far East, the Middle East and North Africa. It is a mixture of recipes gathered on my travels, often only vaguely explained by a gifted but inexact cook after a memorable meal in some far-off place, which I have worked on and put into practice on my return. I also include original ideas of my own which emerged as I learned more and became inspired by a certain type of cuisine.

The recipes are worked out specially to suit an ordinary English kitchen, sometimes modified so as not to startle the taste buds, but always retaining an authentic character and flavour. Any dish can be cooked as part of the normal English meal or, of course, you could put together a completely exotic feast for a special occasion. Personally, I like mixing dishes of quite different styles in one meal; it provides contrast and excitement.

None of the recipes in this book demands particular skills. Because the methods may be unfamiliar I have tried to make the instructions very detailed so that it will be hard to go wrong. In fact, oriental cooking is not difficult. It does not require the exact measurements which many European dishes rely on and you will soon realise that the occasional long list of ingredients consists almost entirely of spices which, once you have them on your shelf, are very little trouble to use. However, before you start

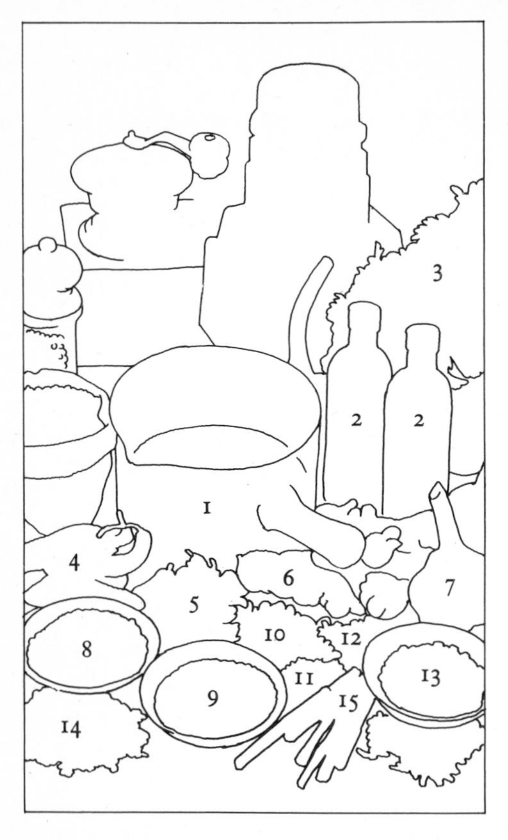

Above and right: *A selection of the spices and other flavourings used in the recipes. (1) Desiccated coconut is infused in milk to produce "coconut milk". (2) Rose water and orange flower water. (3) Coriander leaves. (4) Green chillies. (5) Mace. (6) Fresh ginger. (7) Garlic. (8) Turmeric. (9) Chilli powder. (10) Cardamom pods. (11) Cumin seeds. (12) Cloves. (13) Paprika. (14) Ground coriander. (15) Cinnamon sticks. The coffee grinders, hand-operated and electric, are useful for grinding whole spices to obtain the freshest possible flavour.*

cooking, a few words of advice and explanation about the ingredients, spices and flavourings may prove useful.

Points to remember

Always assemble your ingredients before you start cooking, preparing some in advance if necessary. This makes everything go smoothly and saves you time.

In some of the cooking instructions I have referred to a flame-proof casserole, in which ingredients can be fried on top of the stove and then cooked in the oven. If you don't have one of these, however, you can simply use a frying pan and then transfer the contents to an ordinary casserole.

In several recipes I have specified butter but by far the best thing to use if you can is Sainsbury's Concentrated Butter for Cooking, which is the equivalent of the Indian ghee or clarified butter. It doesn't brown or have any sediment, and will add a rich flavour to the dish. It is also extremely economical and you don't need to use quite as much.

Sunflower oil, which I have specifically mentioned in some of the recipes, is preferable to other oils where ingredients have a delicate taste, as it is more neutral in flavour than other oils; however, any vegetable oil will serve the same purpose.

In all the recipes I have used *ground* spices except where it is specified that you should use them whole. If you can it is better to buy whole spices, as they have an infinitely better flavour when freshly ground. For a particular recipe you can just put the spices you need in an electric coffee grinder and whizz them up within seconds, or grind them in a hand coffee grinder (the coffee you make afterwards will taste extra good!). Alternatively, you can use a pestle and mortar, but this, of course, takes much more time.

The measurements of spices are as I used them, but they are only a rough guide – in India, for instance, no one would ever measure spices. When you do not have all the spices mentioned in a recipe you can experiment as you like. You may find that you prefer the flavour of a certain spice, and you can then try more of it than is specified in the recipe. One of my favourites is cardamom pods. The black seeds must be popped out and the pods discarded before grinding. Their aromatic flavour is exquisite in both savoury and sweet dishes.

Many people think that all oriental food is burning hot. This is by no means so. The hotness is due to the addition of fresh chillies (which also contribute a good flavour), or of chilli powder or cayenne pepper. None of the recipes in this book are very hot, but you can either leave out the chillies completely if you just want an aromatically spiced dish or increase the quantity if you like a more fiery flavour. If a recipe states fresh chillies and you don't have any, use chilli powder or cayenne pepper instead. Fresh chillies keep very well in a plastic bag in the freezer and you can then take one or two out when you need them. It is important to remember that fresh chillies are very strong and after cutting them open you can almost burn yourself if you touch your mouth or eyes. I find the best way is to cut them open under running water, remove the seeds, and then wash your hands thoroughly.

Fresh root ginger gives only a little hotness and a wonderfully refreshing flavour. Many people avoid it because they don't like the taste of ground or preserved ginger, but just cut a piece of root ginger open, smell it and you will realise how different it is. It has an irresistible lemony smell and is an important part of many recipes. As with fresh chillies, it is worth buying a quantity at once, since it is so useful to have but may not be so easy to find. The way to preserve root ginger indefinitely is to put it, peeled and sliced, in a jar with sherry to cover and keep it covered in the fridge or a cool place.

Another flavour which people often do not like but which is quite different used in oriental cooking is coconut. Both the flesh and the milk (which is not the liquid from inside the fresh coconut but the juices which come from soaking fresh grated or desiccated coconut in milk or water) give a mild richness and creaminess to all sorts of dishes. The recipes tell you how to make both thick and thin coconut milk. I was one of those who hated both ginger and coconut but when they are used in Indian and oriental cookery I cannot recommend them enough.

I have included several desserts and sweetmeats which use either rose or orange flower water. These are obtainable from chemists or from specialist shops. I find it best to ask for the triple strength kind, and then use less of it. In any case, it is something you have to taste and judge for yourself.

Finally, I hope that this book will make you realise how very much better oriental dishes are when they are made at home and how exciting and varied this kind of cooking can be.

Note on quantities

Ingredients in the recipes are given in both Imperial (oz, pints, etc) and metric (g, ml, etc) measures: use either set of quantities, but not a mixture of both, in any one recipe. All teaspoons and tablespoons are level unless otherwise stated; metric spoon measures, if you follow these instead, are *always* level.

Curries

Aubergine and Tomato Curry

Serves 4

This goes well with almost any dry curry or with plain roast meat or chicken. It can be eaten as a lunch dish on its own with a simple salad or served cold as a tasty accompaniment to cold meat or fish.

4 long, thin aubergines
salt
1-inch (2.5 cm) piece fresh ginger
2 cloves garlic
1 small green chilli, seeded (optional)
4 tablespoons (4 × 15 ml spoon) vegetable oil
2 teaspoons (2 × 5 ml spoon) ground coriander
1 teaspoon (5 ml spoon) ground cinnamon
½ teaspoon (2.5 ml spoon) ground cloves
14 oz (397 g) tin tomatoes
1 heaped teaspoon (2 × 5 ml spoon) caster sugar

Cut the aubergines into ½-inch (1 cm) rounds, rub with salt and leave in a colander for half an hour (to drain away the bitter juices). Peel the ginger and garlic and chop finely together, with the chilli, if used.

Heat the oil in a heavy saucepan. Fry the ginger, garlic and chilli for a minute or two over medium heat. Add the spices and fry for another minute or so.

Wash the salt thoroughly from the aubergines and pat dry. Add to the saucepan and sauté the aubergines for 2 – 3 minutes. Then add the tomatoes and sugar and bring to bubbling. Cover the pan and simmer very gently, stirring from time to time, for about an hour, until the aubergines are very soft. Season to taste with salt.

Egg and Vegetable Curry

Serves 4–5

Eggs take extremely well to spices and I always find this dish useful for my vegetarian mother-in-law because it is substantial enough to make a main meal, accompanied by a bowl of Basmati Rice (see recipe on p. 45). The cucumber adds a refreshing texture.

2 medium-size aubergines
1-inch (2.5 cm) piece fresh ginger
3–4 cloves garlic
2 tablespoons (2 × 15 ml spoon) oil
2 teaspoons (2 × 5 ml spoon) ground coriander
1 teaspoon (5 ml spoon) ground cinnamon
½ teaspoon (2.5 ml spoon) turmeric
1 teaspoon (5 ml spoon) ground cumin
½ teaspoon (2.5 ml spoon) cayenne pepper
1 large green pepper, sliced
1 small cucumber, sliced in 1-inch (2.5 cm) thick chunks
1 tablespoon (15 ml spoon) lemon juice
14 oz (397 g) tin tomatoes
salt
6 eggs
chopped coriander leaves or parsley to garnish

Cut the aubergines into 2-inch (5 cm) slices, rub all over with salt and leave in a colander for half an hour (to drain away any bitter juices). Peel the ginger and garlic and chop finely together.

Heat the oil in a flame-proof casserole, add the chopped ginger and garlic and the dry spices and fry for a minute or two. Rinse the salt off the aubergines, dry them and add to the casserole with the other vegetables, the lemon juice and the tinned tomatoes. Season with salt. Bring to the boil on top of the stove and then put in the oven at Gas Mark 3/325°F/170°C for about half an hour until the vegetables are very tender.

Meanwhile, boil the eggs semi-hard, shell them and cut them in half. When the curry is cooked add them and put the dish back in the oven for another 5 minutes. Before serving sprinkle with chopped coriander leaves or parsley.

Potatoes in Coconut Milk

Serves 4

One of the best things I ate when I visited Ceylon were potatoes cooked in this way. They are beautifully mild and rich and are a good accompaniment to any dish.

2 oz (50 g) unsweetened desiccated coconut
½ pint (300 ml) milk
1½ lb (675 g) potatoes
1 small green chilli
2–3 small bay leaves
salt
3 × 1-inch (3 × 2.5 cm) sticks cinnamon

Put the coconut in a bowl. Bring the milk to the boil and pour on to the coconut, stir and leave on one side.

Peel the potatoes and cut into smallish pieces. Boil in salted water for 7–10 minutes, until the potatoes are just about cooked but not breaking up, and drain.

Cut open the chilli under running water, discard the seeds and stem and chop the flesh finely. Return the drained potatoes to a saucepan and strain the coconut milk over them through a fine sieve, pressing to extract all the liquid. Add the bay leaves, the chopped chilli, a little salt and the cinnamon sticks. Bring to the boil and simmer for 3 minutes. Transfer to a serving dish.

Spiced Cauliflower

Serves 4

In India they cook vegetables longer than we do so that the spices can penetrate. This dish would go well with any meat or chicken curry and I like it very much with plain roast meat or chicken.

1 largish cauliflower
1-inch (2.5 cm) piece fresh ginger
1 green chilli
4 tablespoons (4 × 15 ml spoon) vegetable oil
salt, to taste
1 rounded teaspoon (2 × 5 ml spoon) sugar
2 teaspoons (2 × 5 ml spoon) ground coriander
1 teaspoon (5 ml spoon) ground cumin
2 tablespoons (2 × 15 ml spoon) lemon juice
a few fresh coriander leaves or a little parsley, chopped, to garnish

Cut the cauliflower into small florets. Peel the ginger. Cut open the chilli under running water and discard the seeds and stem. Finely chop the ginger and chilli together.

Heat the oil in a large heavy saucepan. Add the ginger and chilli and cook over a gentle heat, stirring, for a minute. Add the cauliflower, a sprinkling of salt, the sugar and spices and stir for a minute or two more. Then add the lemon juice, cover the pan tightly and cook gently for 30–40 minutes, stirring now and then and making sure there is just enough liquid in the bottom of the pan to steam the cauliflower.

Turn into a serving dish and sprinkle with the chopped coriander leaves or parsley.

Spiced Cauliflower

Nargis Kofta

Serves 4–5

This is a wonderful dish. As it is mild, the children love it, too, but of course you can add some chilli powder if you like a little fire. One could describe Nargis Kofta as the Indian version of Scotch eggs, only served hot. They are large spiced meatballs encasing a hard-boiled egg and cooked in a rich sauce. Serve with plain or fried rice and either peas or green beans.

½ teaspoon (2.5 ml spoon) ground cloves
1 teaspoon (5 ml spoon) ground cumin
1 teaspoonful (5 ml spoon) ground cinnamon
1¼ lb (600 g) ground or finely minced beef
salt, black pepper
a handful of fresh coriander or mint leaves, chopped
7½ tablespoons (7½ × 15 ml spoon) plain yogurt
2 onions, roughly chopped
1-inch (2.5 cm) piece fresh ginger, peeled and roughly chopped
2–3 cloves garlic, peeled
4 hard-boiled eggs
6 tablespoons (6 × 15 ml spoon) sunflower oil
2 teaspoons (2 × 5 ml spoon) ground coriander
½ teaspoon (2.5 ml spoon) ground turmeric
14 oz (397 g) tin tomatoes
1 heaped teaspoon (2 × 5 ml spoon) paprika

Mix the cloves, cumin and cinnamon into the ground beef in a bowl. Season well with salt and black pepper and add almost all of the chopped coriander or mint and 1½ tablespoons (4 × 5 ml spoon) of the yogurt. Mix together well. Cover the bowl and leave on one side.

Put the onions, ginger and garlic in a liquidiser or food processor with 6 tablespoons (6 × 15 ml spoon) water and whizz to a smooth paste.

Divide the spiced meat into four portions and wrap a portion neatly round each hard-boiled egg. Heat the oil in a large heavy saucepan. Put in the meatballs and turn them carefully until just browned all over (don't worry if they don't brown evenly). Remove them with a slotted spoon and put on a plate.

Add the paste from the liquidiser to the oil left in the pan and fry at medium heat for 8–10 minutes. Then add most of the coriander and turmeric and continue to fry for a minute. Still frying, stir in the remaining 6 tablespoons (6 × 15 ml spoon) of yogurt one spoon at a time and then add the tomatoes, the paprika and salt to taste. Bubble for 2–3 minutes. Add the meatballs, cover the pan and simmer gently for half an hour, turning the meatballs and spooning over the sauce from time to time.

To serve, remove the meatballs with a slotted spoon and cut each in half with a sharp knife. Arrange on a serving dish, pour the sauce over and sprinkle with the remaining chopped coriander.

Spiced Spinach with Eggs and Fresh Ginger

Serves 4

This is a most delicious dish, which you can rustle up for a more exciting lunch or supper. We have it with warm Indian bread or the flat pitta breads which are widely available nowadays.

1¾–2 lb (750–900 g) fresh or frozen spinach
1-inch (2.5 cm) piece fresh ginger, peeled
1 small green chilli, cut open and seeded *or* ¼–½ teaspoon (1.25–2.5 ml spoon) chilli powder
3 large cloves garlic, peeled
2 tablespoons (2 × 15 ml spoon) sunflower oil
2 oz (50 g) butter or margarine
2 heaped teaspoons (4 × 5 ml spoon) ground coriander
1 heaped teaspoon (2 × 5 ml spoon) ground cumin
½ teaspoon (2.5 ml spoon) ground cloves
3 tablespoons (3 × 15 ml spoon) lemon juice
salt
4 large eggs
1 teaspoon (5 ml spoon) paprika

Wash the spinach and remove the stems. Chop the ginger, the seeded chilli and the garlic together finely. Cook the spinach in a little salted water for just a minute or two until limp (if using frozen spinach, simply thaw). Drain the spinach well, pressing out excess water, and cut up finely.

Put a fairly large, shallow serving dish in the oven to get warm. Heat 1 tablespoon (15 ml spoon) oil and 1 oz (25 g) of the butter in a large frying pan. Stir in the chopped ginger, chilli, garlic and spices. Stir over the heat for a minute or two. Then add the spinach and the lemon juice and stir over a gentle heat for 5–8 minutes. Season to taste

with salt and spread the spinach out in the warm serving dish.

Put a tablespoon (15 ml spoon) more oil in the pan and fry the eggs, two at a time, basting with the oil until the white is only just set. Arrange the eggs on the bed of spinach.

Finally melt the remaining 1 oz (25 g) butter in a small saucepan, stir in the paprika and trickle this red liquid over the eggs just before serving.

Chicken Liver Curry

Serves 4

Despite the apparently long list of ingredients, this is a quick, inexpensive and nutritious curry which I find a useful supper dish. It goes well with boiled potatoes and a green salad.

1 lb (450 g) chicken or turkey livers
3 tablespoons (3 × 15 ml spoon) plain yogurt
2 large onions
1–2 green chillies, cut open and with the seeds removed
4 sticks celery, roughly chopped
2 cloves garlic, peeled
1-inch (2.5 cm) piece fresh ginger, peeled
juice of 1 lemon
2 tablespoons (2 × 15 ml spoon) sunflower oil
½ teaspoon (2.5 ml spoon) ground cardamom
1 teaspoon (5 ml spoon) ground cinnamon
½ teaspoon (2.5 ml spoon) ground cloves
1 teaspoon (5 ml spoon) turmeric
2–3 large, juicy tomatoes, sliced
2 tablespoons (2 × 15 ml spoon) tomato purée mixed with
  ½ pint (300 ml) water
salt
chopped parsley to garnish

Cut the chicken livers into 1-inch (2.5 cm) pieces and stir into a bowl with the yogurt. Leave while you prepare the curry sauce.

Roughly chop one of the onions, and put in a food processor or liquidiser with the chillies, celery, garlic, ginger and lemon juice. Blend until as smooth as possible.

Heat the oil in a heavy saucepan and fry the dry spices for a moment; then stir in the blended ingredients. Cover the pan and cook over a very low heat for 15 minutes, stirring quite often. Now slice the remaining onion in rings and add it to the pan together with the chicken livers and yogurt, the tomatoes and the tomato purée and water. Allow to bubble and then turn down the heat and simmer gently for another 15 minutes. Season to taste with salt and spoon into a serving dish; sprinkle with chopped parsley.

Cardamom Fish Curry

Serves 4–5

A mild aromatic dish, very easy to make, with subtle, milky juices which go perfectly with the nutty flavour of Basmati Rice (recipe on p. 45).

$1\frac{1}{2}$–$1\frac{3}{4}$ lb (675–750 g) cod fillet
1 fresh green chilli
2 large cloves garlic
1-inch (2.5 cm) piece fresh ginger
2 tablespoons (2 × 15 ml spoon) sunflower oil
6 cardamom pods
1 medium-size red pepper, sliced thinly in rings
3 oz (75 g) coconut flour *or* 3 oz (75 g) piece creamed coconut
2–3 teaspoons (2–3 × 5 ml spoon) salt
$\frac{1}{2}$ pint (300 ml) boiling water
juice of 1 large lemon
chopped parsley, to garnish

Cut the fish into large chunks. Cut the chilli open under running water and remove the seeds and stem. Peel the garlic and ginger. Chop up the chilli, garlic and ginger together finely.

Heat the oil in a large flame-proof casserole. Stir in the chopped ingredients and the whole cardamom pods. Add the pieces of fish and just seal each side of the fish. Add the red pepper and remove from the heat.

Heat the oven to Gas Mark 3/325°F/170°C. Put the coconut flour and salt into a measuring jug, add the boiling water and stir. Pour this liquid over the fish and add the lemon juice. Bring to bubbling heat, cover the dish and cook in the oven for 30–40 minutes until the fish is cooked. Before serving, sprinkle generously with the chopped parsley.

Cardamom Fish Curry

Nepalese Pork Curry

Serves 4

This is a simply made mild curry with rich, creamy juices. Serve with rice and a green vegetable.

1½ lb (675 g) boneless pork
3 cloves garlic
2 medium-size onions
1 oz (25 g) butter or margarine
1 teaspoon (5 ml spoon) ground cinnamon
1 teaspoon (5 ml spoon) ground coriander
½ teaspoon (2.5 ml spoon) ground cumin
1 teaspoon (5 ml spoon) turmeric
¼ teaspoon (1.25 ml spoon) chilli powder
1 large green pepper, sliced
a little over ¼ pint (150 ml) water
8 oz (225 g) curd cheese
salt
a handful of chives, chopped

Cut the meat into largish cubes. Peel the garlic and onions and chop very finely.

Heat the oven to Gas Mark 3/325°F/170°C. Melt the butter in a flame-proof casserole and fry the onion and garlic over medium heat for 2–3 minutes, stirring. Stir in the dry spices. Add a little more butter if quite dry and add the meat, stirring until it is sealed all over. Add the sliced pepper and the water and season with salt. Add the curd cheese and stir until melted.

Bring to bubbling, cover and cook in the oven for 1–1½ hours until the meat is tender. Before serving sprinkle with chopped chives.

Samosas

Serves 4

These crispy triangles filled with spiced minced beef disappear in a flash when I present a plate of them to my family. In India samosas tend to be very hot but the children won't eat anything too "peppery", and so this is a mild version which we all prefer. Like Cornish pasties, samosas take a little time to prepare but as with pasties you can make them well in advance and cook them when you want them; or you can cook them earlier and then reheat them. Serve them with a bowl of plain yogurt and chopped mint, which you can use as a dipping sauce.

For the dough
4 oz (100 g) plain or wholewheat flour
1 teaspoon (5 ml spoon) baking powder
½ teaspoon (2.5 ml spoon) salt
1½ tablespoons (4 × 5 ml spoon) sunflower or vegetable oil
2–3 fl oz (50–80 ml) water

For the filling
1 onion
1 tablespoon (15 ml spoon) oil
½ teaspoon (2.5 ml spoon) ground cloves
2 teaspoons (2 × 5 ml spoon) ground cinnamon
2 teaspoons (2 × 5 ml spoon) ground cumin
¼–½ teaspoon (1.25–2.5 ml spoon) chilli powder
1 teaspoon (5 ml spoon) ground turmeric (optional)
2 cloves garlic, chopped finely
½ lb (225 g) minced beef
1 rounded tablespoon (2 × 15 ml spoon) tomato purée
2 tablespoons (2 × 15 ml spoon) lemon juice
1 rounded tablespoon (2 × 15 ml spoon) frozen peas,
  thawed (optional)
salt

oil for deep frying

To make the dough, mix the flour, baking powder and salt in a bowl. Mix in the oil. Mix in the water, a little at a time until you have a firm dough which leaves the sides of the bowl clean. Knead the dough on a floured board with the palm of your hand for 5–8 minutes until smooth. Form into a ball, brush with a little oil, cover and set on one side while you make the filling.

To make the filling, peel the onion and chop into small pieces. Heat the oil in a frying pan and cook the onion until just soft. Add the dry spices and the garlic and stir. Then add the beef, breaking it up and stirring over a medium heat for 5–8 minutes until cooked. Add the tomato purée and lemon juice, and the peas, if used, and cook for about 2 more minutes. Remove from the heat and add salt to taste. Allow the mixture to cool.

Meanwhile, divide the dough into 13–15 equal pieces. Form the pieces into balls, flatten them and roll out thinly on a floured surface into circles 3–4 inches (7.5–10 cm) in diameter. Cut the circles in half with a sharp knife. Moisten half the cut edge of each circle, fold in half and press the cut edge over to seal and so form a wide cone.

Cup each cone open in your hand and spoon three-quarters full with the meat mixture. Dampen the edges and press over again to seal completely. Deep fry in hot oil in batches until golden brown (3–4 minutes), removing with a slotted spoon and draining on kitchen paper.

Moghul Chicken

Serves 6

This is my simple-to-make version of an elaborate dish eaten on feast days in India. The mildly spiced chicken has a thick, rich almond and coconut sauce. Serve with Basmati Rice and a vegetable curry such as Aubergine and Tomato Curry, and perhaps a bowl of Yogurt with Cucumber and Mint to refresh the palate (see pp. 45, 11 and 44).

2 oz (50 g) desiccated coconut
2 oz (50 g) blanched almonds
½ pint (300 ml) hot water
1-inch (2.5 cm) piece fresh ginger, peeled
½ teaspoon (2.5 ml spoon) chilli powder
2 large onions
3 oz (75 g) butter or margarine
6 chicken joints
6–8 whole cardamom pods, lightly crushed
2 × 2–3-inch (2 × 5–7.5 cm) sticks cinnamon
6 whole cloves
6 tablespoons (6 × 15 ml spoon) plain yogurt
salt
1 oz (25 g) flaked almonds
a few chopped coriander leaves or a little chopped parsley, to garnish

Put the coconut, blanched almonds, peeled ginger and chilli powder into a liquidiser, add the hot water and whizz until smooth.

Peel and slice the onions into rings. Heat the butter in a flame-proof casserole, add the onions and fry over moderate heat until soft and golden.

Heat the oven to Gas Mark 4/350°F/180°C. Add the mixture from the liquidiser to the casserole and stir. Add the chicken joints, the whole spices and the yogurt and season with salt. Mix thoroughly over the heat, then cover the dish and cook in the oven, stirring occasionally for 1½–2 hours until the chicken is very tender.

Just before serving fry the flaked almonds in a little butter for a minute until golden, and sprinkle over the top, together with chopped coriander leaves or parsley.

Rabbit Curry with Eggs

Serves 4

Boneless Chinese rabbit is inexpensive and cooks well with spices and in curries. In this recipe for a mild curry the combination of coconut and curd cheese gives a rich creamy sauce with a tang of yogurt added at the end. Spiced Cauliflower (recipe p. 14) is a good accompaniment.

2 oz (50 g) desiccated coconut
½ pint (300 ml) boiling water
2–3 cloves garlic
2 tablespoons (2 × 15 ml spoon) sunflower oil
1 lb (450 g) boneless rabbit
½ teaspoon (2.5 ml spoon) ground cardamom
2 teaspoons (2 × 5 ml spoon) ground cinnamon
¼–½ teaspoon (1.25–2.5 ml spoon) chilli powder
4 large hard-boiled eggs, sliced thickly
2 large ripe tomatoes, sliced
4 oz (100 g) curd cheese
3–4 tablespoons (3–4 × 15 ml spoon) plain yogurt
salt

Put the desiccated coconut into a bowl, pour over the boiling water and leave to soak for 10 minutes or more.

Peel and chop the garlic finely. Heat the oil in a pan and stir in the rabbit pieces, adding the spices, chilli powder and chopped garlic. Stir over a gentle heat for 2–3 minutes and then transfer to a casserole dish, adding the sliced eggs and tomatoes.

Strain the liquid from the coconut into another bowl, pressing the coconut to extract all its juices. Then stir the curd cheese into this coconut milk until more or less dissolved. Pour this mixture into the casserole dish.

Heat the oven to Gas Mark 8–9/450°–475°F/230°–240°C and put the covered casserole into the oven for 15–20 minutes until bubbling. Then turn down the heat to Gas Mark 4/350°F/180°C for about 45 minutes or until the rabbit is tender. Season to taste with salt and add a pinch more chilli if you like a hotter flavour. Before serving, stir in the yogurt.

Sweetbreads in Curried Butter Sauce

Serves 4

When I was travelling in India I always searched for brain curry on the menu as it can be a most exquisite dish. As brains are less easy to come by I have tried out my own version with lamb's sweetbreads. It is simple to make, mild and tender; the sweetbreads and butter magically combine to make their own rich creamy sauce with a zest of fresh ginger and chilli. Serve with plain rice and a crisp green vegetable so as not to detract from the delicate flavour.

1 lb (450 g) lamb's sweetbreads
1 tablespoon (15 ml spoon) vinegar
1-inch (2.5 cm) piece of fresh ginger
1 green chilli
2 large onions
3 oz (75 g) butter or margarine
salt
coriander leaves or parsley, chopped, to garnish

Soak the sweetbreads in water for an hour or two, changing the water once or twice to get rid of all traces of blood. For the final half-hour of soaking add the vinegar to the water.

Peel the ginger and cut the chilli open under running water, discarding the stalk and seeds. Chop the ginger and chilli together finely. Peel the onion and slice in rings.

Melt 2 oz (50 g) of the butter in a large, heavy frying pan and fry the onions over a medium heat. When the onions are soft and golden, add the chopped ginger and chilli and fry, stirring, for about a minute. Add the remaining 1 oz (25 g) of butter and turn the heat to as low as possible. Drain the sweetbreads and add them to the pan. Put a piece of foil or a lid over the pan and cook, stirring occasionally, for 10–15 minutes. Season to taste with salt and transfer to a warm serving dish (if necessary cover the dish and keep warm in a very low oven until you are ready to eat). Just before serving sprinkle with the chopped coriander leaves or parsley.

Lamb Fillets Cooked in Spinach

Serves 4

This North Indian curry is one of my favourites. The tender pieces of lamb are enveloped in spinach leaves, richly spiced but not hot (though you can add a chilli if you wish). I like it best served with rice and a salad of crisp lettuce, green peppers and spring onions. A bowl of Yogurt with Cucumber and Mint (see recipe on p. 44) also goes well with it.

1 lb (450 g) fresh spinach (or frozen spinach leaves, thawed and drained)
1 large onion
3–4 cloves garlic
1-inch (2.5 cm) piece fresh ginger
3 tablespoons (3 × 15 ml spoon) water
1¼–1½ lb (550–675 g) lamb neck fillets (or other boneless lamb)
3 tablespoons (3 × 15 ml spoon) vegetable oil
½ teaspoon (2.5 ml spoon) ground cloves
2 teaspoons (2 × 5 ml spoon) ground coriander
2 teaspoons (2 × 5 ml spoon) ground cinnamon
½ teaspoon (2.5 ml spoon) ground cardamom
1 teaspoon (5 ml spoon) ground turmeric
1 teaspoon (5 ml spoon) ground cumin
1 tomato, chopped finely
3 tablespoons (3 × 15 ml spoon) plain yogurt
salt
a handful of fresh coriander leaves or parsley, chopped, to garnish

Wash and pick the stalks off the spinach and push down into a very little boiling water, just until the leaves wilt. Run under cold water, drain and chop up roughly. Peel and roughly chop the onion, garlic and ginger, put into a blender or food processor with the water and whizz to a smooth paste.

Cut the lamb into 2-inch (5 cm) pieces. Heat the oil in

a flame-proof casserole (or a large frying pan) and fry the meat over a high heat just to brown all over. Remove the meat with a slotted spoon and set aside.

Heat the oven to Gas Mark 4/350°F/180°C. Lower the heat to medium and add the paste from the blender to the casserole. Then, still stirring, add the dry spices and the chopped tomato. Cook for 2–3 minutes, stirring. Stir in the yogurt and add the browned lamb and a generous sprinkling of salt. Finally stir in the chopped spinach.

Cover the dish and cook in the oven for about an hour until the meat is tender. This curry is supposed to be a "dry" curry, which means cooked with no extra juices (like a stew) but if you think it looks too dry you can always add a little water. Just before serving, sprinkle with the coriander leaves or parsley.

Beef Curry with Almond Sauce

Serves 6

This dish transforms even the cheapest stewing beef; cooked until it is meltingly tender in a richly spiced thick dark sauce it is a dish fit for any occasion. I prefer to do without rice and cook two contrasting vegetables instead, such as carrots and spinach. Don't be too put off by the long list of ingredients – it is just a few more spices than usual, and you can leave out any that you don't have.

2 lb (900 g) stewing beef
4 tablespoons (4 × 15 ml spoon) vegetable oil
1 teaspoon (5 ml spoon) ground cardamom
½ teaspoon (2.5 ml spoon) ground cloves
1 teaspoon (5 ml spoon) ground black pepper
2 teaspoons (2 × 5 ml spoon) ground cumin seeds
3 teaspoons (3 × 5 ml spoon) ground coriander seeds
½ teaspoon (2.5 ml spoon) ground turmeric
3 oz (75 g) blanched almonds
1 rounded tablespoon (2 × 15 ml spoon) desiccated coconut
1-inch (2.5 cm) piece fresh ginger, peeled and roughly chopped
6 cloves garlic, peeled and roughly chopped
2 onions, finely chopped
6 tablespoons (6 × 15 ml spoon) plain yogurt
14 oz (397 g) tin tomatoes
salt
chilli powder, to taste
a few coriander leaves or a little parsley, chopped, to garnish

Cut the beef into bite-size cubes. Heat 3 tablespoons (3 × 15 ml spoon) of the oil in a large, deep frying pan and fry the beef all over to brown. Transfer the beef to a casserole, leaving the oil in the pan.

Put all the dry spices in the frying pan and fry for a minute or two, stirring. Add the almonds and coconut and continue to fry, still stirring, until the nuts are well browned. Spoon the mixture into a liquidiser and add the chopped ginger and garlic and 6 tablespoons (6 × 15 ml spoon) water. Whizz to a smooth thick paste, pushing it down a little if necessary.

Add the remaining tablespoon (15 ml spoon) oil to the pan you fried the meat in. Fry the chopped onions over a high heat, stirring, until dark brown. Then turn down the heat and stir in the paste from the blender and 3 tablespoons (3 × 15 ml spoon) of the yogurt. Add the tinned tomatoes and their juices and ¼ pint (150 ml) water. Simmer gently for 2–3 minutes.

Turn off the heat and add salt and a little chilli powder to taste. Pour the sauce over the meat, cover and bring to bubbling.

Cook in the oven at Gas Mark 1–2/275–300°F/140–150°C for 2–3 hours until the meat is very tender, stirring once or twice during the cooking. Before serving, spoon on the remaining 3 tablespoons (3 × 15 ml spoon) yogurt and sprinkle with the coriander leaves or parsley.

Parsi Chicken Curry with Matchstick Chips

Serves 4

I first watched this dish being made in the tiny kitchen of some Parsi friends in Calcutta. My children love it for its topping of matchstick chips. Garam masala, used in this dish, is a ready-made mixture of Indian spices which is available in small tins.

2 tablespoons (2 × 15 ml spoon) sunflower oil
4 onions
2–3 cloves garlic, chopped finely
1–2 fresh or dried red chillies
1 teaspoon (5 ml spoon) garam masala
4 chicken joints
8 dried apricots
4 oz (100 g) chicken livers
1–2 packets Crunchy Sticks
salt

Heat the oil in a large, heavy saucepan. Slice the onions finely, put half in the saucepan and just soften over a gentle heat. Fry the remaining onion in a frying pan until golden brown and leave the pan on one side.

Add the garlic and whole chillies to the saucepan and stir in the garam masala. Then add the chicken joints and enough hot water to half cover the chicken. Add salt, cover the saucepan and simmer on top of the stove for about 20 minutes. Add the dried apricots, the chicken livers and the pre-fried onions. Continue to simmer gently for half an hour longer, until the meat starts to leave the bone.

Warm the Crunchy Sticks and a serving dish in the oven. Transfer the chicken and juices to the serving dish and just before serving sprinkle with Crunchy Sticks on top.

Chutneys and Other Curry Accompaniments

Yogurt with Aubergine, Mint and Cumin

Serves 4–6

This is a refreshing side dish, suitable as an accompaniment to any meat or chicken curry.

1 smallish aubergine
1–3 tablespoons (1–3 × 15 ml spoon) sunflower oil
1 clove garlic, finely chopped
1 teaspoon (5 ml spoon) ground cumin
1 lb (500 g) carton plain yogurt
salt
a pinch of cayenne pepper
a small handful of fresh mint leaves, finely chopped

Slice the aubergine across in rings and then into semicircles. Rub the pieces all over with salt and leave in a colander in the sink for half an hour (to drain away the bitter juices). Then wash the salt off the aubergine and pat dry.

Heat the oil in a frying pan. Add the aubergine and fry over medium heat until soft. Then add the chopped garlic and the cumin. Stir and cook for another 2–3 minutes. Turn off the heat and leave to cool.

Empty the yogurt into a bowl. Add salt and the cayenne pepper. Stir in the aubergine, scraping every bit of oil and spice from the pan. Then stir in the chopped mint leaves, leaving a few for garnish on top. Keep in the fridge until needed.

Fresh Mint Chutney with Coconut

This refreshing chutney will keep in a cupboard or in a container in the fridge for a week or so. It is good with lamb or fish and also in the recipes that follow for potato balls or baked aubergines. If you can get fresh coriander leaves instead of mint for the chutney it will be even better.

a large handful of fresh mint leaves
flesh of 1 fresh coconut, grated
1 heaped teaspoon (2 × 5 ml spoon) cumin seeds
6 cloves garlic
1–2 green chillies, with the seeds removed
1 teaspoon (5 ml spoon) sugar
2 teaspoons (2 × 5 ml spoon) salt
2 tablespoons (2 × 15 ml spoon) lemon juice

Simply put all the ingredients in a food processor or liquidiser and whizz up until smooth.

Mint Chutney Potato Balls

This is a good way to use up left-over mashed potato. The stuffed potato balls are delicious served instead of roast potatoes with lamb, pork or chicken.

cold mashed potato
Fresh Mint Chutney with Coconut
1 egg, beaten
browned breadcrumbs
oil for deep frying

Form the mashed potato into balls about the size of ping-pong balls. Make a hole with the end of a wooden spoon in each and put in a little mint chutney. Seal over with potato. Dip the balls in the egg and then in the bread-crumbs and deep fry until golden.

Fresh Mint Chutney with Coconut, together with Baked Aubergines with Fresh Mint Chutney and Mint Chutney Potato Balls

Baked Aubergines with Fresh Mint Chutney

Serves 4

I adore these as a first course, either hot or cold.

4 small aubergines
Fresh Mint Chutney with Coconut
oil
salt

Cut the aubergines in half lengthways and rub the flesh with salt. Leave in a colander for half an hour to drain away the bitter juices. Then rinse off the salt and smear the cut side of the aubergines with mint chutney. Put them together again, smear the outsides well with oil and put closely together in an oven-proof dish, so that they don't fall apart.

Cover the dish with oiled foil. Heat the oven to Gas Mark 4/350°F/180°C and cook the aubergines for $\frac{3}{4}$–1 hour – depending on their size – until they are soft and a small sharp knife slides in easily.

Fresh Mint Chutney with Apple and Orange

If you have a liquidiser or food processor fresh uncooked chutneys take minutes to make and are quite a different thing from the thicker and heavier cooked chutneys. They have a very refreshing taste and will keep in a covered jar in the fridge for a week or so. You can serve this mint chutney with any dry curry, with kebabs and meatballs or as a welcome variation to mint sauce with roast lamb. It is also good with cold meat and irresistible with bread and cheese.

a good handful of fresh mint leaves
½ green pepper, roughly chopped
1 medium orange, peeled, pipped and cut up roughly
1 sharp apple, peeled, cored and cut up roughly
juice of ½ lemon
¼–½ teaspoon (1.25–2.5 ml spoon) cayenne pepper
1 teaspoon (5 ml spoon) salt

Simply whizz all the ingredients to a paste in a liquidiser or food processor – adding more mint leaves if it seems too liquid, though it is supposed to be a wet chutney.

Onion and Orange Chutney

A buttercup-yellow, translucent chutney which goes particularly well with game, pork or gammon. Because of its beautiful appearance it is perfect for presents and for stalls at school bazaars, etc.

1–2 red chillies
6–8 cloves garlic
4–5 large onions
3 large oranges
½ lb (225 g) granulated sugar
10 whole cardamom pods, lightly crushed
1 teaspoon (5 ml spoon) ground turmeric
½ pint (300 ml) white wine vinegar
½ pint (300 ml) water

Cut open the chillies under running water and remove the seeds and stems. Peel the garlic and chop finely together with the chillies. Peel and chop the onions into ½-inch (1 cm) pieces. Squeeze the juice out of the oranges into a heavy saucepan. Scrape the pith out of the orange shells with a teaspoon, cut the peel into small pieces and add to the saucepan together with the chopped garlic and chillies and all the remaining ingredients.

Stir together, bring to the boil and then simmer gently, uncovered, for about 1½ hours, stirring occasionally at first and more often as the mixture thickens. Spoon into jam jars when cool and keep in the fridge or a cool place.

Sweet Tomato Chutney

This is a delicious sweet and sour chutney, made very easily at any time of the year with tinned tomatoes. It is a mild chutney and goes well with any curry, and, of course, with cold meat or bread and cheese. It keeps well in the fridge for months.

8 cloves garlic, peeled and coarsely chopped
2-inch (5 cm) piece fresh ginger, peeled and coarsely chopped
½ pint (300 ml) wine vinegar
2 × 14 oz (397 g) tin tomatoes
¾ lb (350 g) granulated sugar
2 tablespoons (2 × 15 ml spoon) sultanas
2 teaspoons (2 × 5 ml spoon) salt
2 tablespoons (2 × 15 ml spoon) flaked almonds
¼–¾ teaspoon (1–3 × 1.25 ml spoon) cayenne pepper to taste

Put the chopped garlic and ginger with a little of the vinegar in a liquidiser and whizz until smooth. Empty the tomatoes and their juices, the rest of the vinegar, the sugar, the sultanas and the salt into a heavy saucepan. Bring to the boil and add the garlic and ginger mixture.

Lower the heat and simmer gently, uncovered, for 1½–1¾ hours, stirring occasionally at first and more as the mixture thickens. Finally add the flaked almonds and cayenne pepper to taste. Leave to cool, then bottle and keep in the fridge.

Onion and Orange Chutney, Sweet Tomato Chutney

Yogurt with Cucumber and Mint

A refreshing side dish to go with all curries.

1 small cucumber
a handful of fresh mint leaves
1 lb (500 g) carton yogurt
$\frac{1}{4}$–$\frac{1}{2}$ teaspoon (1.25–2.5 ml spoon) cayenne pepper
salt

Peel the cucumber and either grate or chop into little cubes. Chop the mint leaves finely. Put the yogurt into a pretty bowl and season with cayenne pepper and salt to taste. Stir in the cucumber and mint. Chill in the fridge and eat the same day.

Pilau Rice

Serves 4–5

This rice can be served with all kinds of Indian and oriental dishes. With Turkish or North African dishes you can add 1 oz (25 g) currants and 2 teaspoons (2 × 5 ml spoon) dried dill with the onions and omit the turmeric, giving you white rice instead of yellow. For Indian dishes add a little ground cinnamon with the turmeric.

2 onions
6 oz (150 g) long-grain easy-cook rice
1 tablespoon (15 ml spoon) sunflower oil
1 oz (25 g) butter
$\frac{1}{2}$ teaspoon (2.5 ml spoon) turmeric
6 fl oz (180 ml) water
salt, cayenne pepper

Peel the onions and chop into small pieces. Put the rice into a sieve and wash thoroughly under hot running water.
Melt the oil and butter in a heavy-based saucepan and

add the turmeric and the onions. Season with salt and a pinch or two of cayenne pepper and cook gently until the onion is just soft. Then stir in the washed rice and add the water. Cover the pan and simmer gently for 8–12 minutes – until all the liquid has been absorbed and the rice is cooked but still has a slight bite to it. Using a fork, transfer to a serving dish.

Basmati Rice with Whole Spices

Serves 5–6

Basmati rice is smaller than ordinary long-grain rice and has a delicious, nutty flavour, far superior to any other rice. Cooked in this way the rice is delicately aromatic and goes well with endless dishes. If you want to colour it yellow, add turmeric with the whole spices. If basmati rice is unobtainable use ordinary long-grain rice and cook for a little longer.

8 oz (225 g) basmati rice
1 tablespoon (15 ml spoon) sunflower oil
1 oz (25 g) butter
5–8 whole cardamom pods
3 × 2-inch (3 × 5 cm) sticks cinnamon
½ teaspoon (2.5 ml spoon) turmeric (optional, for colour)
a little over ½ pint (300 ml) water
1 teaspoon (5 ml spoon) salt

Put the rice into a sieve and wash through well with cold water. Then put it into a bowl with 1 pint (600 ml) salted water, soak for half an hour and drain.

Heat the oil and butter in a saucepan, add the whole spices (and turmeric, if required) and stir for a moment;

then add the drained rice. Pour in the water and stir in the salt.

Bring to the boil, cover tightly and reduce the heat to as low as possible (this is important) for 12–16 minutes until the rice is tender but still has a very slight bite to it. Using a fork, turn out on to a warm serving dish.

Bhatura Bread

Makes approx. 14

A puffed-up, deep-fried bread specially good with tandoori dishes and grilled meats but also delicious to mop up the juices of curry. Once the dough is made, you can keep it in the fridge and use it as you want it.

8 oz (225 g) strong white or wholemeal flour
2 tablespoons (2 × 15 ml spoon) plain yogurt
1 teaspoon (5 ml spoon) baking powder
1 rounded teaspoon (2 × 5 ml spoon) salt
½–1 teaspoon (2.5–5 ml spoon) chilli powder
oil for deep frying

Mix the ingredients with sufficient warm water to make a stiff dough, either with a wooden spoon or the dough hook of an electric mixer, until it leaves the sides of the bowl. (If it is still sticky, add a little more flour.) Knead well, form into a ball and leave covered at room temperature for 4–6 hours.

Roll the dough into a fat sausage and cut off ¼–½-inch (0.5–1 cm) rounds. Roll out each round on a floured surface to the size of a saucer. Deep fry the bhaturas quickly in smoking oil, patting down gently (so that they puff up) and turning once. Eat as soon as possible, though, if you have to, you can keep them warm in a low oven.

Chapatis and Bhatura Bread

Chapatis

Makes approx. 14

Chapatis are the simplest form of wholemeal Indian bread and are eaten with almost all the curries. You tear bits off them and use them as a scoop for mopping up the juices. They are fun to make and my children love them spread with butter and jam for tea!

8 oz (225 g) wholewheat flour
1 teaspoon (5 ml spoon) salt
about ¼ pint (150 ml) water
oil

Put the flour and salt into a bowl. Add enough water to form a rather soft and sticky dough. Knead well for 8–10 minutes, folding and kneading with the palm of the hand. Cover the dough with a damp cloth and leave to rest for at least half an hour.

Knead the dough again, form into balls the size of ping-pong balls, flatten slightly and dip in a little more of the wholewheat flour. Roll out each piece of dough on a well floured board as thinly as you can. (This is easier if you dip the chapati into flour from time to time, as otherwise the dough tends to stick.)

Lightly oil a heavy frying pan or griddle and set over a medium heat. Cook the chapatis one at a time, turning with a palette knife when you see bubbles appearing and then cooking the other side until they puff up more. Pile them on a plate, and when they are all cooked cover with foil and keep warm in a very low oven until ready to eat.

More Oriental Dishes

Chinese Egg Soup

Serves 4

A Chinese meal is not complete without a clear, delicate broth. This simple soup makes an excellent first course to any meal, stimulating the appetite without being too filling.

2 × 14½ oz (411 g) tin consommé *or* 1½ pints (825 ml) light chicken stock
3 spring onions, sliced in small pieces
½-inch (1 cm) piece fresh ginger, peeled
a little sherry (optional)
1 egg
2 tablespoons (2 × 15 ml spoon) finely shredded Chinese leaves or Cos lettuce

Put the stock in a saucepan with the spring onions and ginger. Bring to the boil, cover and simmer for 20 minutes.

Remove the ginger, season to taste with salt and a little pepper and add a little sherry, if liked. Then put back on the heat and bring to a rolling boil. Break in the whole egg and mix in with a fork to break up into strands. Lastly add the shredded Chinese leaves or lettuce, bubble for a minute more and serve.

Crunchy Stir-fried Vegetables

Serves 6–8

This is a wonderful mixture of vegetables which will go well with almost anything and is particularly good with roast chicken. The dish will keep warm in a low oven without spoiling for a short time before serving. In China, all cooking of this kind is done in a *wok*, which can now be bought in England; however, a large deep frying pan works well.

1 lb (450 g) white cabbage
1 medium-size turnip
2 tablespoons (2 × 15 ml spoon) sunflower oil
1 oz (25 g) butter or margarine
½ lb (225 g) fresh bean sprouts (optional)
2 oz (50 g) mushrooms, sliced
1 tablespoon (15 ml spoon) caster sugar
soy sauce
salt (optional)

Slice the cabbage finely. Peel the turnip, cut it in half and slice into very fine semi-circles.

Heat the oil and butter or margarine in a large, deep frying pan or iron casserole dish. Add the sliced cabbage and fry, stirring over a medium heat for 3–5 minutes, until just beginning to soften. Add the slices of turnip and stir for another minute or so. Then add the bean sprouts, if used, and mushrooms (and more oil and butter if necessary) and cook for another minute.

Finally, stir in the sugar and a very generous sprinkling of soy sauce. Cook for another minute or two. Taste and add a little salt if required.

Crunchy Stir-fried Vegetables

Carrots in Sweet and Sour Sauce

Serves approx. 4

This is an enhancing accompaniment to bacon or roast pork but also good served cold as a relish with cold pork, ham or chicken.

1 lb (450 g) carrots
2 tablespoons (2 × 15 ml spoon) sunflower oil
salt
½ pint (300 ml) water
1 tablespoon (15 ml spoon) cornflour
1 rounded tablespoon (2 × 15 ml spoon) sugar
1 tablespoon (15 ml spoon) soy sauce
1 tablespoon (15 ml spoon) wine vinegar
chopped spring onions, to garnish

Wash and scrape the carrots and cut into small cubes, approx. ½ inch (1 cm). Heat the oil in a large, heavy pan. Fry the carrots, stirring for 2–3 minutes. Then season generously with salt, add ¼ pint (150 ml) of the water and simmer gently until the carrots are tender.

In a bowl mix the cornflour, sugar, soy sauce and vinegar with the remaining ¼ pint (150 ml) water until smooth. Add to the carrots, bring to the boil and bubble until the sauce is thick and translucent. Turn into a serving dish and before serving sprinkle with the chopped spring onions.

Exotic Fish Pie

Serves 6

If you like fish pie you will welcome any variations. This is far removed from nursery fish pie, yet in our house it is just as popular, even with the children. Serve it simply with a salad.

1½ lb (675 g) potatoes
1¾ lb (800 g) skinned cod or whiting fillets
1 large red pepper
1 large onion
2 oz (50 g) butter
3 tablespoons (3 × 15 ml spoon) vegetable oil
1-inch (2.5 cm) piece fresh ginger
3 cloves garlic
1 red or green chilli
4 tablespoons (4 × 15 ml spoon) plain yogurt
2 teaspoons (2 × 5 ml spoon) ground cinnamon
salt

Boil the potatoes and cut into round slices. Cut the fish into 1½-inch (3.5 cm) chunks. Cut the red pepper and the onion into 1-inch (2.5 cm) pieces.

Melt 1 oz (25 g) of the butter and 1 tablespoon (15 ml spoon) of the oil in a large frying pan. Fry the pepper and onion very gently until soft.

Meanwhile peel the ginger and garlic and cut the chilli open under running water, discarding the seeds and stem. Chop the ginger, garlic and chilli together very finely. Remove the pepper and onion from the pan, using a slotted spoon, and put into a large, fairly deep dish in a very cool oven to keep warm.

Add another tablespoon (15 ml spoon) of oil to the pan and heat to medium heat. Put in the fish and spices and cook, turning the pieces gently once or twice, for 5–7 minutes. Sprinkle with salt and add the yogurt. Allow the yogurt to become just hot, but not to boil, and then pour the contents of the pan into the serving dish and mix with the pepper and onion.

Finally, heat the remaining 1 oz (25 g) butter and tablespoon (15 ml spoon) oil in the pan and add the cinnamon and sliced potatoes. Fry, stirring the potatoes, for about 5 minutes. Top the fish with the fried potatoes and serve.

Golden Orient Eggs

Serves 3–4

I think these are quite delicious. The hard-boiled eggs are covered in a golden yellow sauce made with rich coconut milk, flavoured with onion and tomato and spiced with turmeric and chilli. They make a perfect supper or lunch dish, accompanied simply by a green vegetable such as broccoli and with Basmati Rice (see recipe on p. 45).

4 oz (100 g) unsweetened desiccated coconut
1 pint (600 ml) milk
6–8 eggs
1 medium-size onion
1 clove garlic
1 large, squashy tomato
1 oz (25 g) butter or margarine
1 teaspoon (5 ml spoon) ground turmeric
½–1 teaspoon (2.5–5 ml spoon) chilli powder
salt
finely chopped spring onions, to garnish

Put the coconut in a bowl. Bring the milk to the boil, pour on to the coconut, stir, and leave for about 20 minutes.

Meanwhile boil the eggs medium hard, shell them and cut them in half. Peel and finely chop the onion and

garlic. Pour boiling water over the tomato, skin it and chop finely.

Melt the butter or margarine in a frying pan, add the onion and garlic and cook gently, stirring around until soft and golden. Then add the tomato and cook until softened.

Strain the milk from the coconut into a jug through a fine sieve, pressing to extract all the liquid. Gradually stir the milk into the frying pan mixture. Add the turmeric and the chilli powder, and salt to taste. Bring to the boil and bubble for a minute. Pour the mixture into a liquidiser or food processor and whizz until smooth.

Return the sauce to the pan and add the halved eggs. Bubble gently for 2–3 minutes and then put into a warm serving dish. Just before serving sprinkle on the spring onions.

Rolled Beef with Cheese, Sage and Garlic

Serves 6–8

This is a delicious way of cooking stewing beef, both easy and quite fun to make. The mingling of flavours, with the melted cheese, is unusual and very good. I usually serve layered potatoes and onions cooked in the oven with this, together with a green vegetable.

2 lb (900 g) stewing beef, cut into thin slices
a handful of fresh sage leaves
3 large cloves garlic, peeled
6 oz (150 g) Jarlsberg or Edam cheese
tomato purée
salt, black pepper
1 large glass red wine
1 heaped tablespoon (2 × 15 ml spoon) cornflour
5 oz (150 g) carton soured cream

Lay out the pieces of beef. Chop the sage and garlic together very finely. Slice the cheese thinly into as many slices as there are of beef. Smear each piece of beef generously with tomato purée and sprinkle with salt and pepper. Lay on a slice of cheese and then pat on the finely chopped sage and garlic. Roll each piece of beef over and secure with a toothpick.

Lay the beef rolls in a flame-proof casserole dish. Heat the oven to Gas Mark 2/300°F/150°C. Pour over the red wine and enough water to three-quarters cover the beef. Bring to the boil on top of the stove and then cover and cook in the oven for 1¾–2 hours, until the meat feels tender when you stick a knife into it.

Drain the juices from the meat into a saucepan. Mix the cornflour with a little water until smooth and add to the juices. Bring to the boil, stirring, and bubble for 3–4 minutes. Pour the sauce back over the beef and spoon the soured cream over the top before serving.

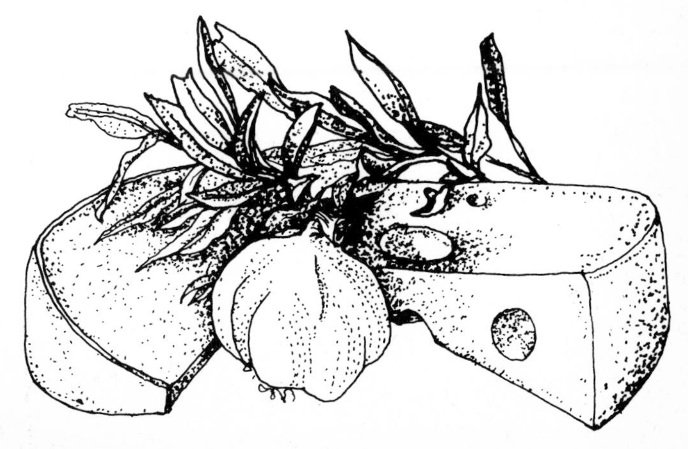

Fish in Cabbage Leaves with Curd Cheese and Mustard

Serves 4

In the Far East this delicate and delicious dish would be cooked in banana leaves, which impart a subtle flavour of their own, but in this country a good alternative is to use cabbage leaves. A tomato salad or baby carrots are a perfect accompaniment.

4 large cabbage leaves
4 oz (100 g) curd cheese
4 tablespoons (4 × 15 ml spoon) whole seed mustard
1 teaspoon (5 ml spoon) salt
black pepper
4 small fillets cod or whiting
a few fresh coriander leaves or a little parsley, chopped, to garnish

Plunge the cabbage leaves in boiling salted water for 2 minutes. Mix the curd cheese with the mustard, salt and pepper. Smear the mixture on both sides of the fillets (rolling them up into a compact shape if necessary) and wrap each fillet up in a cabbage leaf, tying up neatly with string or cotton.

Steam the fish for 20–30 minutes, depending on its thickness. (If you have no steamer, put the fish in a colander over a large pan of boiling water and cover.) Put the fish parcels in a serving dish, dot with butter, sprinkle with the chopped coriander or parsley and serve.

Fish in Cabbage Leaves with Curd Cheese and Mustard

Fillets of Fish with Soft Roe Sauce and Cashew Nuts

Serves 6–8

In this dish the fish is cooked in mild coconut milk, and just a zest of mace and chilli, and then served under the creamy blanket of a sauce made with soft herring roes topped with golden cashew nuts. I hope this gives an idea of how good it tastes. New potatoes and baby carrots are ideal with this dish.

½ pint (300 ml) milk
2 oz (50 g) desiccated coconut
4 blades mace
1–2 dried red chillies, broken up roughly
2 lb (900 g) cod or whiting fillets
a good blob of butter
6 oz (150 g) soft herring roes (fresh or tinned)
1 tablespoon (15 ml spoon) lemon juice
2 oz (50 g) plain cashew nuts

First bring the milk to the boil in a saucepan with the coconut, the mace and the broken chillies. (If you don't like too hot a flavour, remove any seeds first.) Simmer gently for about 5 minutes and then cover the pan, remove from the heat and let stand to infuse for about half an hour.

Cut the fish into large pieces and lay in a fairly shallow ovenproof dish. Heat the oven to Gas Mark 6/400°F/200°C. Strain the milk through a sieve on to the fish and cover the dish with foil. Bake in the centre of the oven for 25–30 minutes until the fish is lightly cooked. Pour the juices from the fish into a bowl and keep the fish warm in a very cool oven.

Melt the butter in a frying pan and fry the herring roes lightly for a few minutes until cooked. Sprinkle with salt. Add the roes and their buttery juice to the milky juices the fish has cooked in and put in a liquidiser or food processor with the lemon juice. Whizz until smooth. Test the sauce for seasoning and pour it over the fish (if the sauce is not still hot, reheat it in a pan first). Melt a little butter in a pan and fry the cashew nuts for about a minute until golden. Sprinkle them over the top of the dish and serve.

Honey Pork Tagine

Serves 4–5

In Morocco there are countless varieties of tagine, a kind of spiced stew with deliciously concentrated juices. Many of them are slightly sweet, cooked with honey, nuts and dried fruit. In England we are used to eating pork with sweet things and I find this tagine is very popular. Serve with plain boiled rice and a green salad.

1 heaped teaspoon (2 × 5 ml spoon) ground mace or nutmeg
1 heaped teaspoon (2 × 5 ml spoon) ground cinnamon
1 teaspoon (5 ml spoon) ground ginger
¼ pint (150 ml) water
1½–2 lb (675–900 g) boneless pork shoulder steaks
3 oz (75 g) large stoneless raisins
2 oz (50 g) butter or margarine
1 onion, chopped finely
2 oz (50 g) blanched almonds
2 tablespoons (2 × 15 ml spoon) lemon juice
salt
2 tablespoons (2 × 15 ml spoon) honey
chopped parsley or celery leaves, to garnish

Stir the spices into the water. Heat the oven to Gas Mark 9/475°F/240°C. Put the shoulder steaks into a casserole dish and pour over half the spiced water. Put the raisins into the remaining water and leave to soak.

Add the butter or margarine, chopped onion, almonds,

lemon juice and a little salt to the casserole. Cover and cook in the centre of the oven for about 20 minutes or until the juices are bubbling; then lower the heat to Gas Mark 4/350°F/180°C for 1 hour.

Add the raisins and spiced water and stir in the honey. Put back in the oven for a further ½–¾ hour or until the pork is very tender.

Strain the juices from the casserole into a saucepan and boil up fiercely for 3–4 minutes until reduced to a thick and shiny sauce. Pour this back into the casserole over the meat, almonds and raisins. Sprinkle with a little chopped parsley just before serving.

Veal in Almond and Sweet Pepper Sauce

Serves 4

This is an easy dish to make, with a most beautiful orange colour and a rich flavour which mingles best with plain boiled rice and a crisp green vegetable such as broccoli or very lightly cooked beans.

2 oz (50 g) blanched almonds
2 tablespoons (2 × 15 ml spoon) desiccated coconut
1 large red pepper
2 red chillies
2 oz (50 g) butter or margarine
2 teaspoons (2 × 5 ml spoon) paprika
1 rounded teaspoon (2 × 5 ml spoon) caster sugar
3 tablespoons (3 × 15 ml spoon) lemon juice
½ pint (300 ml) hot water
1 lb (450 g) pie veal – cut into cubes
2 heaped tablespoons (4 × 15 ml spoon) plain yogurt
spring onions or parsley, finely chopped, to garnish

Grind up the almonds and coconut in a coffee grinder or in

Veal in Almond and Sweet Pepper Sauce

a liquidiser. Slice the red pepper into smallish pieces, removing the seeds, and cut the chillies in half under running water, discarding the seeds and stems.

Melt the butter in a frying pan and cook the red pepper and chillies gently until soft. Then remove from the pan and put into a liquidiser or food processor with the ground almonds and coconut, paprika, caster sugar and lemon juice. Blend together and then add the hot water, a little at a time, to make a sauce. Add salt to taste.

Heat the oven to Gas Mark 4/350°F/180°C. Fry the veal pieces in the remaining pan fat over a medium heat for about 5 minutes, turning to seal all over. Stir in the prepared sauce and bubble for a minute or two. Transfer immediately to a casserole dish.

Cover and cook for about 1 hour or until the meat is tender. Before serving spoon the yogurt on top and sprinkle with the spring onions or parsley.

Cinnamon Chicken with Sweet Onion Sauce

Serves 4

In this North African dish joints of chicken are cooked under a blanket of sweet, translucent onions in a glossy sauce. I like to serve it with brown rice or pearl barley, and broad beans or peas go well with it.

4 large onions
4 chicken joints
3 oz (75 g) butter or margarine
1½ teaspoons (3 × 2.5 ml spoon) ground cinnamon
¼ pint (150 ml) water
1 rounded tablespoon (2 × 15 ml spoon) soft brown sugar
salt, black pepper
chopped fresh mint, to garnish

Peel the onions and slice in fairly thick rings. Put the onion and chicken joints in a large saucepan with the butter or margarine, cinnamon and water. Season with salt and pepper. Heat gently until the butter has melted, then bring to the boil, cover the pan and simmer for about 5 minutes.

Heat the oven to Gas Mark 6/400°F/200°C and put in an ovenproof dish to warm. Remove the chicken joints from the saucepan with a slotted spoon and put into the ovenproof dish. Add the sugar to the onion and liquid in the saucepan and stir thoroughly. Spoon the onion on top of the chicken joints and pour the liquid over. Cook uncovered in the centre of the oven for 35–45 minutes, basting often.

Strain all the liquid from the dish into a saucepan and season it with more salt, if required. Rearrange the chicken joints on the dish, pile the onion on top and put the dish in a very low oven to keep warm. Then bring the liquid to the boil and boil fiercely for 4–5 minutes until it becomes a really thick and syrupy sauce. Spoon this sauce over the chicken and onion just before serving and sprinkle on a little chopped fresh mint.

Chinese Money Bags

Serves 4

Or in other words, stuffed dumplings – but we always call them money bags because that is what they look like. They are thin, pancake-like dumplings filled with well flavoured pork and pepper and then steamed. I like to serve them with either sliced leeks or cabbage, fried gently in butter until soft and used as a border to the dumplings.

For the dough
8 oz (225 g) plain flour
1 teaspoon (5 ml spoon) salt
3 teaspoons (3 × 5 ml spoon) caster sugar
2 teaspoons (2 × 5 ml spoon) baking powder
¼ pint (150 ml) cold water

For the filling
1 lb (450 g) minced pork
1 large green pepper, chopped finely
2–3 cloves garlic, chopped finely
2 tablespoons (2 × 15 ml spoon) white wine vinegar
2 teaspoons (2 × 5 ml spoon) anchovy essence (optional)
soy sauce
salt and black pepper

To make the dough, sift the flour, salt, caster sugar and baking powder into a bowl and mix in the cold water to form a smooth dough which leaves the sides of the bowl. Cover the dough while you prepare the filling.

Put the minced pork into a bowl and add the chopped pepper and garlic. Stir in the vinegar, the anchovy essence, a generous sprinkling of soy sauce, salt and black pepper.

Turn the dough on to a floured board and knead for a few minutes until smooth and pliable. Tear off pieces of dough and form into balls the size of a large marble. Roll

each to a thin circle with a rolling pin. Put a tablespoon (15 ml spoon) of the filling in each circle and pull the dough up round it, pinching well to seal. (The dumplings should be very full to avoid too much dough at the top.)

Rub the dumplings all over with oil. Steam over boiling water for 20 minutes. (If you have no steamer use either a collapsible vegetable steamer or a colander in a large covered saucepan.) Take the dumplings out carefully with a spoon, arrange on a serving dish and sprinkle with soy sauce just before serving.

Peking Pork with Mushrooms and Cashew Nuts

Serves 4–5

Once you have prepared your ingredients, Chinese stir-fried dishes are made within minutes, and both flavour and texture benefit from such short cooking. Serve this dish with rice or Chinese noodles and some finely sliced white cabbage, lightly cooked.

¾–1 lb (350–450 g) pork tenderloin
1 tablespoon (15 ml spoon) sherry
2 tablespoons (2 × 15 ml spoon) soy sauce
¼–½ teaspoon (1.25–2.5 ml spoon) chilli powder
1 tablespoon (15 ml spoon) caster sugar
3 tablespoons (3 × 15 ml spoon) sunflower oil
6 oz (150 g) mushrooms, sliced finely
1 rounded teaspoon (2 × 5 ml spoon) cornflour
3 tablespoons (3 × 15 ml spoon) water
1 bunch spring onions, chopped
2 oz (50 g) cashew nuts

Using a sharp knife cut the tenderloin crossways into very thin slices. Put them into a bowl with the sherry, 1 tablespoon (15 ml spoon) of the soy sauce, the chilli powder and the caster sugar and mix together thoroughly.

Heat 2 tablespoons (2 × 15 ml spoon) of the sunflower oil in a pan and when very hot add the meat and stir continuously for 2 minutes. Remove the meat with a slotted spoon and leave on a plate on one side.

Stir the mushrooms in a bowl with the remaining soy sauce. Heat the remaining tablespoon (15 ml spoon) of oil with the juices in the frying pan and stir the mushrooms for half a minute. Return the meat to the pan and remove from heat.

Stir the cornflour in a cup with the water until smooth and add to the pan mixture. Put back on gentle heat, stir for a minute or two until the juices are thickened and then add the spring onions and cashew nuts, continuing to stir for another minute. Transfer the mixture to a warm serving dish.

Doner Kebabs

Serves 4

The best doner kebabs in Turkey come from the pretty town of Borsa on the far side of the Sea of Marmara. In spite of the many take-away kebab restaurants which have sprung up in England, nothing tastes like the succulent, aromatic lamb of Borsa. But my children adore doner kebabs stuffed into unleavened pitta bread so I have contrived this quick and easy imitation to make at home.

1 lb (450 g) lamb, minced
3 cloves garlic, chopped finely
1 tablespoon (15 ml spoon) whole wheat flour
2 tablespoons (2 × 15 ml spoon) oil
2 teaspoons (2 × 5 ml spoon) ground cumin
3 teaspoons (3 × 5 ml spoon) ground coriander
2 teaspoons (2 × 5 ml spoon) ground cinnamon
1 egg, beaten
salt, black pepper
4 pitta breads
a handful of fresh mint
1 small onion
wedges of lemon

Grind the lamb very finely in a food processor or put through a mincer, three times if possible. Put into a bowl and add the chopped garlic, flour, oil, spices and egg, and a generous seasoning of salt and black pepper. Mix all together thoroughly with a wooden spoon.

Spread the mixture out on to a large baking sheet (this has to go under the grill, and so if you have a small grill you may have to do the meat in two halves using a smaller baking sheet). Press the meat down with your hands to make a thin, even layer all over the baking sheet.

Wrap the pitta breads in foil and heat in a moderate

oven. Chop up the mint leaves fairly roughly and slice the onion into the finest possible rings.

Heat the grill. Put the meat under a hot grill for about 4–5 minutes until it is browned and somewhat shrunken. Then turn the meat over, using a wide spatula and your hands. Grill the other side for a further 4–5 minutes. Then cut the meat into thin strips.

With a sharp knife cut the pitta breads down the side, using your hands to open them up like a pocket. Stuff each bread with pieces of meat and the chopped mint and slices of onion. Serve with wedges of lemon to squeeze over the meat before eating.

Apricot Duck with Cashew Nuts

Serves 4

Although not much trouble to make, this is a most delicious dish and very festive-looking with its dark, shiny sauce and scattering of golden nuts. Plain, long-grain brown rice and a green vegetable go well with it.

4 joints duck (or 1 duck, jointed)
4–5 tablespoons (4–5 × 15 ml spoon) plain yogurt
2 large cloves garlic, chopped finely
3 heaped teaspoons (6 × 5 ml spoon) paprika
¾ teaspoon (3 × 1.25 ml spoon) cayenne or chilli powder
a little oil for frying
3 oz (75 g) dried apricots
1 large wineglass apple juice or sweet cider
soy sauce
2 oz (50 g) cashew nuts or blanched almonds
chopped fresh coriander leaves, parsley or mint, to garnish

If the duck joints are very big, cut them in half. Mix the

yogurt with the garlic, paprika and cayenne pepper or chilli powder. Rub the joints all over with this mixture and if possible leave for several hours to absorb the flavours.

Heat a very little oil in a large frying pan and fry the joints on both sides, just to brown. Transfer them to a large saucepan with the dried apricots. Pour over the apple juice and about ½ pint (300 ml) water, enough to three-quarters cover the duck. Sprinkle generously with soy sauce. Bring to the boil, then cover and simmer for ¾–1 hour until the duck is tender.

Remove the joints of duck and all the apricots and arrange on a serving dish. Keep warm in a low oven. Boil up the remaining juices fiercely until much reduced and thickened, and test for seasoning. Fry the cashew nuts or almonds in a little oil for a moment until golden. Just before serving pour the thickened sauce over the duck and sprinkle with the nuts and the coriander, parsley or mint.

Crystal Chicken

Serves 4–6

This effortless Chinese way of cooking a chicken to eat cold produces a pure white bird of perfect texture and delicate flavour which carves easily into thin, moist slices. The chicken actually cooks by just sitting in water which has been brought to the boil for a moment only. There can surely be no more gentle or fuel-saving method of cooking. It is very important, however, to use a *fresh*, not frozen, chicken, to avoid the possibility of undercooking.

3–3½ lb (1.35–1.5 kg) fresh roasting chicken
just over 3 tablespoons (3 × 15 ml spoon) white wine vinegar
1 onion, peeled and sliced roughly
3–4 slices fresh ginger, approx. ¼ inch (0.5 cm) thick
1 bunch spring onions, chopped
soy sauce

Rub the chicken all over with a little of the vinegar. Insert four metal skewers through the body and legs of the chicken to act as heat conductors.

Put enough water to cover the chicken (but not the chicken itself) into a large, heavy saucepan. Add the 3 tablespoons (3 × 15 ml spoon) of vinegar to the water and bring to a fast boil. Put in the onion, ginger and the chicken and bring to the boil again for half a minute. Cover the pan, turn off the heat and leave the chicken in the water until it gets completely cold. The chicken will then be cooked.

Chill the drained chicken in the fridge. To serve, carve in very thin slices and arrange on a dish. Scatter with chopped spring onions and just before serving sprinkle with streaks of soy sauce.

Crystal Chicken

Meatballs Cooked in Yogurt

Serves 4

These mildly spiced meatballs in a delicious, tangy yogurt sauce are easy to make and very popular. They are typical of Turkish and Middle Eastern cookery. Serve with rice and a firm vegetable such as beans, peas or carrots.

2–3 large cloves garlic
1¼ lb (600 g) minced lamb (or beef)
2 teaspoons (2 × 5 ml spoon) ground cinnamon
1 teaspoon (5 ml spoon) ground mace
3 heaped teaspoons (6 × 15 ml spoon) paprika
a handful of chopped mint leaves or parsley
salt
½–1 teaspoon (2.5–5 ml spoon) cayenne pepper
1 egg, whisked
2 tablespoons (2 × 15 ml spoon) vegetable oil
1 tablespoon (15 ml spoon) cornflour
¼ pint (150 ml) milk
5 oz (150 ml) carton plain yogurt

Peel the garlic and chop finely. Put the minced meat in a bowl and add the garlic, spices and all but a little of the chopped mint or parsley. Mix well and season with plenty of salt and the cayenne pepper, and then mix in the whisked egg. Using wet hands, form into walnut-size balls.

Heat the oil in a large frying pan and fry the meatballs over a high heat just to brown all over. Turn off the heat. Mix the cornflour in a cup with 2 tablespoons (2 × 15 ml spoon) of the milk until smooth. Pour into a flame-proof casserole or heavy saucepan. Stir in the yogurt and then add the remaining milk. Season with salt and a pinch or two of cayenne pepper. Bring to the boil, put in the meatballs, cover the casserole and simmer gently on top of the stove for 15–20 minutes. Just before serving sprinkle the remaining mint or parsley on top.

Marinated Kidney Kebabs

Serves 4

The marination makes these spiced lamb's kidneys meltingly tender, and are ideal for a barbecue. They are good served with rice and a green vegetable such as spinach. Those who prefer a hotter dish should use the larger amount of cayenne shown below.

12 lamb's kidneys
2 tablespoons (2 × 15 ml spoon) vinegar
4 tablespoons (4 × 15 ml spoon) plain yogurt
1 teaspoon (5 ml spoon) ground cumin
1 teaspoon (5 ml spoon) ground cinnamon
1–2 teaspoons (1–2 × 5 ml spoon) cayenne pepper
salt (preferably sea salt)

Cut the kidneys across into quarters. Put into a bowl, cover with water and stir in the vinegar. Leave for an hour or so.

Drain and pour away the water. Now put the yogurt in the bowl and stir the spices into it. Mix in the kidneys and leave for another hour or more.

Thread the kidneys on to long skewers. Spoon the yogurt marinade over them and cook under a hot grill (or barbecue) for 5–8 minutes each side until they look slightly charred. Sprinkle salt on them when you serve them and scrape up all the marinade juices, which will taste delicious.

Grilled Chicken Strips, Indian Style

Serves 4

The taste of these tender, marinated pieces of chicken breast is sublime. Children love them. Everyone loves them. They are simple to prepare and equally good hot or cold, so you can take them on picnics. They are also ideal for outdoor cooking. If you have them hot, eat them with rice and perhaps a bowl of Yogurt with Cucumber and Mint (see p. 44) and a vegetable. If eaten cold, serve salads with them. If you find you don't have all the spices needed for the marinade, simply add a little more of the ones you do have.

1¼–1½ lb (550-675 g) chicken or turkey breast, boneless and skinless

For the marinade
1 small onion, sliced roughly
1-inch (2.5 cm) piece of fresh ginger, peeled and chopped roughly
6–8 cloves garlic, peeled
3 teaspoons (3 × 5 ml spoon) ground coriander
2 teaspoons (2 × 5 ml spoon) ground cumin
2 teaspoons (2 × 5 ml spoon) ground cinnamon
1 teaspoon (5 ml spoon) ground cardamom
½ teaspoon (2.5 ml spoon) ground cloves
½ teaspoon (2.5 ml spoon) cayenne pepper
3 tablespoons (3 × 15 ml spoon) red wine vinegar
3 tablespoons (3 × 15 ml spoon) sunflower oil
1 tablespoon (15 ml spoon) tomato purée
1 rounded teaspoon (2 × 5 ml spoon) salt

Slice the chicken breast into thin strips, about ½ inch (1 cm) wide, and put in a bowl. Then simply put all the marinade ingredients into a liquidiser and whizz to a smooth paste. Mix the marinade very thoroughly with the

chicken strips, cover the bowl and leave in a cool place or in the fridge for 4 hours or more (overnight if convenient).

Set the grill to the highest heat. Spread the chicken pieces on a baking sheet (you may have to cook them in two batches if your grill is small) and grill for 8–10 minutes on each side, until almost black in patches.

Crispy Chicken with Sweet and Sour Sauce

Serves 4

This is a quickly made dish which children seem to love. The golden chicken pieces look so enticing under their coating of glossy dark sauce. Serve with plain boiled rice and either a green salad or finely sliced white cabbage fried in butter and sprinkled with soy sauce.

4 chicken joints
2 cloves garlic, finely chopped
salt, black pepper
5 tablespoons (5 × 15 ml spoon) wine vinegar
oil for deep frying
3 tablespoons (3 × 15 ml spoon) honey
1 tablespoon (15 ml spoon) soy sauce
2 teaspoons (2 × 5 ml spoon) cornflour
2 tablespoons (2 × 15 ml spoon) water
chopped spring onions, to garnish

Put the chicken joints into a saucepan with enough hot water just to cover them. Cover the pan, bring to the boil and simmer for 10 minutes. Strain off the water (you can keep this to use as stock) and add the garlic, a good seasoning of salt and black pepper and the wine vinegar to the chicken in the pan. Cover the pan again and simmer gently for another 5 minutes. Then remove the chicken joints, leaving the juices in the pan.

Heat the oil in a deep pan and fry the chicken over a high heat until golden brown all over. Drain the joints, put into a serving dish and keep warm while you make the sauce.

Add the honey and soy sauce to the juices in the saucepan and stir until the honey is melted. Stir the cornflour into the 2 tablespoons (2 × 15 ml spoon) water and add to the pan juices. Bring to the boil and bubble gently, stirring, for 2–3 minutes. Spoon the sauce over the chicken joints just before serving and sprinkle some chopped spring onions on top.

Pork with Crispy Noodles

Serves 4

In this recipe thin, tasty pieces of pork tenderloin, mixed with fresh ginger and crisp scarlet and white radishes, are piled on to a nest of crispy noodles. It is always popular with children.

4 oz (100 g) Chinese noodles
oil for deep frying
2 cloves garlic
1-inch (2.5 cm) piece fresh ginger
¾ lb (350 g) pork tenderloin
1 bunch radishes
1 tablespoon (15 ml spoon) sunflower oil
salt
1 rounded tablespoon (2 × 15 ml spoon) caster sugar
soy sauce
scant tablespoon (15 ml spoon) white wine vinegar
spring onions, chopped, to garnish

Boil the noodles in salted water for 6–8 minutes. Rinse under cold water and drain. Put a large round shallow serving dish in a low oven to warm.

Heat the oil in a deep pan until smoking. Put in the boiled noodles and fry at high heat until golden brown and crisp. Lift out with a slotted spoon and drain on absorbent paper. Spread the noodles in the serving dish and keep warm in the oven.

Peel the garlic and ginger and chop up together finely. Slice both the pork tenderloin and the radishes very finely. Heat the sunflower oil in a frying pan and fry the garlic and ginger over a medium heat for 1 minute. Turn up the heat, putting in a little more oil if necessary, and add the slices of pork and fry, stirring often, for 5–8 minutes until the pork is cooked. Add a sprinkling of salt, the sugar, a generous sprinkling of soy sauce and the vinegar.

Lastly, stir in the radishes and toss over the heat for a minute. Spoon the pork mixture on to the centre of the crispy noodles and sprinkle with chopped spring onions just before serving.

Pork, Onions and Mushrooms in Crispy Batter

Serves 4–5

I have arrived at this dish, which everyone seems to love, by a devious route. It is both Chinese and Japanese in idea but the batter made with beer, which is what makes it so light and crispy, is something I had at a friend's house in Turkey. (Try the batter also with pieces of fish, mussels or prawns and other raw vegetables – it is mouthwatering!) Serve a simple salad with this – I don't think it needs anything else.

$\frac{3}{4}$ lb (350 g) belly of pork rashers
1 tablespoon (15 ml spoon) soy sauce
2–3 pinches cayenne pepper
2 small onions, sliced finely in rings
3 oz (75 g) mushrooms, sliced

For the batter
4 oz (100 g) self-raising flour
1 teaspoon (5 ml spoon) salt
1 small egg
$\frac{1}{4}$ pint (150 ml) beer (any kind)
oil for deep frying

Cut the skin off the pork rashers, cut them into approximately 1-inch (2.5 cm) squares and put into a steamer or sieve suspended over boiling water in a covered saucepan. Steam for 10–15 minutes, until the pork is cooked.

Put the pork in a bowl and stir in the soy sauce and cayenne pepper. Leave to cool a little. Then add the sliced onions and mushrooms.

To make the batter sift the flour and salt into a bowl, mix in the egg and gradually add the beer. Beat until smooth (or simply whizz all the ingredients up in a liquidiser or food processor). Leave the batter for 20 minutes or so.

Heat the oil in a large, deep pan until smoking. Empty the batter into the bowl of pork and vegetables and stir to coat thoroughly. Fry over a high heat in batches until golden brown, separating the pieces as much as possible and draining on absorbent kitchen paper. Pile on a plate and serve immediately.

Lamb in Walnut and Orange Sauce

Serves 4

In Turkey the large plump walnuts arranged in elaborate patterns on the market stalls are the finest I have ever seen. They use them for cooking in all sorts of ways and in this recipe the nuts add richness and subtlety to a simple dish. It is served on a bed of Pilau Rice (see p. 44).

$\frac{1}{2}$–$\frac{3}{4}$ lb (225–350 g) lamb neck fillet or other boneless lamb
2 onions
3 largish tomatoes
2 oz (50 g) butter
grated rind and juice of 1 orange
2 oz (50 g) finely chopped walnuts
salt, black pepper
a handful of Cos lettuce leaves, chopped
a grating of whole nutmeg

Slice the lamb and the onions into small dice. Pour boiling water over the tomatoes, skin them and chop up into small pieces.

Melt the butter in a heavy-based saucepan. Add the lamb and onions and stir with a wooden spoon over a high heat to seal. Add the orange rind and juice, walnuts and tomato. Season with salt and black pepper.

Cover the pan and simmer very gently, stirring occasionally, for $\frac{1}{2}$–$\frac{3}{4}$ hour until the meat is tender. Then add the chopped lettuce and cook for another 5 minutes. Pile in the centre of a bed of rice and grate a little whole nutmeg over both the meat and the rice before serving.

Turkey with Cucumber and Cashew Nuts in Anchovy Sauce

Serves 4

This is quickly made and extremely good. The slices of turkey breast and peeled cucumber are lightly poached in stock and then, together with the crunchy cashew nuts, lie under a tasty anchovy sauce. It is an ideal dish for weight watchers too, served simply with lightly steamed shredded cabbage sprinkled with soy sauce. For those not so conscious of their weight it is excellent with soft egg noodles. A hint of anchovy flavour is used in poultry and pork dishes to great effect in the Far East.

1 lb (450 g) skinned and boned turkey breast
1 fairly small cucumber
1 chicken stock cube
1½ pints (825 ml) water
1 clove garlic, chopped finely
1-inch (2.5 cm) piece of fresh ginger, peeled and finely chopped
2 oz (50 g) plain cashew nuts
a knob of butter
1 tablespoon (15 ml spoon) cornflour
3 teaspoons (3 × 5 ml spoon) anchovy essence
soy sauce
salt, black pepper
spring onions, to garnish

Slice the turkey fillets thinly. Peel the cucumber, cut in half, then into quarters and finally into 2-inch (5 cm) strips.

Dissolve the chicken cube in the water in a largish saucepan, add the chopped garlic and ginger and bring to the boil. Drop in the pieces of cucumber and return to the boil for 5 minutes. Lift out the cucumber with a slotted spoon and put into a warm serving dish.

Bring the stock to the boil again, add the turkey slices

and boil gently for another 5 minutes. Take out the slices, again using a slotted spoon, and add to the cucumber.

Fry the cashew nuts gently in the butter for a minute or two just until golden and add to the dish. Dissolve the cornflour in a little water and stir into the stock. Bring to the boil and bubble for about 3 minutes. Add the anchovy essence and a generous sprinkling of soy sauce. Add salt and pepper to taste if required. Strain the sauce through a sieve on to the turkey and cucumber (if necessary, cover the dish and keep warm in a very low oven until ready to eat). Before serving, chop the spring onions finely, using as much of the green stalk as you can, and sprinkle on top of the sauce.

Sweetmeats and Desserts

Golden Fingers

Makes 18

All over the Middle East you find different ways of making these fingers. My version has a curd cheese filling flavoured with almonds, orange and cinnamon, soaked in a refreshingly sharp orange flower water syrup. They go very well with a salad of fresh orange slices or with plain yogurt.

For the dough
4 oz (100 g) strong plain flour
1 teaspoon (5 ml spoon) salt
2 teaspoons (2 × 5 ml spoon) baking powder
2 teaspoons (2 × 5 ml spoon) caster sugar

For the filling
6 oz (150 g) curd cheese
1 teaspoon (5 ml spoon) caster sugar
1 oz (25 g) sweet almonds, roughly ground
½ teaspoon (2.5 ml spoon) ground cinnamon
finely grated rind of 1 orange

For the syrup
¾ lb (350 g) granulated sugar
8 fl oz (225 ml) water
1 tablespoon (15 ml spoon) strong orange flower water
3 tablespoons (3 × 15 ml spoon) lemon juice

oil for deep frying

Sift the flour, salt, baking powder and caster sugar into a bowl and add enough water (2–3 fl oz, 50–80 ml) to form a smooth stiff dough which leaves the sides of the bowl. Cover the dough and leave in the fridge while you prepare the filling.

Soften the curd cheese in a bowl with the caster sugar. Stir in the almonds, cinnamon and orange rind. Divide the dough in half and roll out one half on a well-floured board until it is very thin, lifting it up often to make sure plenty of flour is underneath. It should look almost transparent. With a sharp knife cut into approximately 3-inch (7.5 cm) squares. Spoon a good teaspoon (5 ml spoon) of the filling on the top of each square, folding the sides over the filling and rolling up like little sausages. Moisten the ends to seal. When the first half of the dough is used up knead the left-over bits into the second piece and repeat the process until all the filling is used up.

Now make the syrup. Dissolve the granulated sugar in the water in a saucepan over a gentle heat. Then bring to the boil and boil fiercely for 3 minutes. Turn off the heat and stir in the orange flower water and lemon juice.

Heat the oil in a deep pan until smoking. Turn down the heat to medium. Fry a batch of fingers, removing them with a slotted spoon when golden brown and putting into the hot syrup. While you fry the next batch take the cooked ones out of the syrup and put on to a plate to cool. When they are all done put them in a serving bowl (glass looks pretty), and when the syrup has cooled pour it on to the fingers through a fine sieve.

Persian Honey Cakes

Makes approx. 16

This is an adaptation of an old Persian recipe. The nutty orange-flavoured cakes are left to absorb a scented honey syrup. You can serve them either for tea, with coffee or as an after-dinner sweetmeat. As a dessert they are excellent with plain yogurt.

8 oz (225 g) fine semolina
2 oz (50 g) icing sugar, sifted
4 fl oz (110 ml) sunflower oil
grated rind and juice of 1 orange
2 oz (50 g) self-raising flour
½ teaspoon (2.5 ml spoon) baking powder
½ teaspoon (2.5 ml spoon) ground cinnamon

For the syrup
4 oz (100 g) sugar
4 tablespoons (4 × 15 ml spoon) honey
5 tablespoons (5 × 15 ml spoon) triple strength orange flower or rose water
¼ pint (150 ml) water

Put the semolina and icing sugar into a bowl. Heat the oil in a saucepan and pour it over the semolina. Stir well and then mix in the orange rind and juice and the flour sifted with the baking powder and cinnamon.

Heat the oven to Gas Mark 3/325°F/170°C. Take up pieces of dough about the size of a ping-pong ball and form short sausage shapes, about 2 inches (5 cm) long. Arrange slightly apart on a large oiled baking sheet. Bake in the centre of the oven for 35–50 minutes.

While the cakes are baking, make the syrup. Put the sugar, honey, flower water and water into a saucepan. Dissolve the sugar and honey over a low heat and then boil fiercely for 4–5 minutes. When the cakes are baked, lift them with a spatula and arrange closely together in a large shallow dish. Pour the syrup over them and leave for several hours, spooning the syrup over them occasionally. Then carefully pile the cakes on a plate, scraping up any remaining syrup and spooning it over.

Gulab Jamun

Makes 24

There are countless varieties of sweets in India but these golden milky balls in rosewater syrup are often the only ones to be found in Indian restaurants in England. However, they are far better made at home and provide a perfect ending even to a completely British meal. My children adore their squeaky texture. They can be made at least a day in advance.

8 oz (225 g) dried milk (such as Sainsbury's "Easy Pints")
1 tablespoon (15 ml spoon) plain flour
1 tablespoon (15 ml spoon) baking powder
about $\frac{1}{4}$ pint (150 ml) milk
oil for deep frying
8 oz (225 g) sugar
$\frac{1}{2}$ pint (300 ml) water
approx. 2 tablespoons (2×15 ml spoon) rose water, to taste

Sieve together the milk powder, the flour and the baking powder. Add enough milk to make a stiff dough and leave to stand for an hour.

Roll the dough between your palms into walnut-size balls. Heat oil in a deep pan until medium hot, not smoking, and fry the balls until they expand and are a rich golden brown all over. (The oil must not get too hot or the balls will become brown too quickly without cooking properly inside.) Drain the balls on some absorbent paper.

Meanwhile, make a syrup by dissolving the sugar in the water and then boiling fiercely for 2–3 minutes. Then add the rose water. Put the cooked balls into a bowl – they look best in a glass bowl – and pour the hot syrup over them. Allow to soak for a few hours before serving.

Gulab Jamun and Persian Honey Cakes

Kheer

Serves 3–4

Kheer could be described as Indian rice pudding. It is far removed from the slab of white stodge often served as rice pudding in England. Kheer is an aromatic luxury pudding made with concentrated creamy milk and nuts and flavoured with rose water and cardamom.

6 whole cardamom pods
1 pint (550 ml) milk
4 oz (100 g) dried milk (such as Sainsbury's "Easy Pints")
1 rounded tablespoon (2 × 15 ml spoon) long-grain rice
1 rounded tablespoon (2 × 15 ml spoon) caster sugar
2–4 teaspoons (2–4 × 5 ml spoon) rose water
1 oz (25 g) flaked almonds

Put the cardamom pods into a heavy pan with the milk. Heat the milk and stir in the dried milk. Add the rice. Bring to the boil and simmer very gently for half an hour, stirring often. Then discard the cardamom pods and stir in the caster sugar, the rose water and three-quarters of the almonds. Spoon into individual dishes and sprinkle the remaining almonds on top. Leave to cool, then refrigerate until needed.

Casablanca Cakes

Makes 30

My children adore these Moroccan delights. They are half-cake, half-biscuit, and are extremely quick and easy to make. They are crunchy and gooey at the same time, with the flavour of almond, lemon and a hint of orange flower water.

1 large egg
just over 4 oz (100 g) icing sugar
½ teaspoon (2.5 ml spoon) baking powder
2 oz (50 g) ground almonds
4 oz (100 g) semolina
finely grated rind of 1 lemon
triple strength orange flower water (optional)

Whisk the egg with 4 oz (100 g) icing sugar until very pale. Stir in the baking powder, ground almonds, semolina and lemon rind and mix thoroughly together.

Heat the oven to Gas Mark 4/350°F/180°C. Grease a large baking sheet and put out a small bowl of sieved icing sugar. Wet your hands with the orange flower water (or with plain water), take up pieces of the mixture and form into balls the size of large marbles, dipping one side of each ball into the icing sugar. Then place the balls on the baking sheet, sugar side up and well spaced out as they spread quite a bit. You will probably have to cook them in two batches. Bake in the centre of the oven for 10–12 minutes until very pale brown. Ease the biscuits off the baking sheet carefully with a palette knife and cool on a rack.

Almond Dreams with Lychees

Serves 6

Wonderfully refreshing after a rich meal, this is an easy-to-make Chinese dessert. Almond Dreams are translucent white, softly jellied squares with a delicate flavour of almond. They look strange and beautiful in a bowl, topped with scented lychees under a glossy syrup. (If you dislike the flavour of almond omit the essence and add 1 tablespoon (15 ml spoon) strong rose water to the liquid before cooling.)

2 × ½ oz (2 × 15 g) packets gelatine
¾ pint (425 ml) milk
3 tablespoons (3 × 15 ml spoon) sugar
½ teaspoon (2.5 ml spoon) almond essence
2 × 11 oz (2 × 275 g) tin lychees

For the syrup
1 tablespoon (15 ml spoon) lemon juice
4 oz (100 g) sugar

Lightly oil a cake tin or roasting pan about 9 inches × 9 inches (23 cm × 23 cm) large. Put the gelatine into a bowl with 4 tablespoons (4 × 15 ml spoon) water and put the bowl over a saucepan of very hot water. Stir until dissolved.

In another saucepan heat 1 pint (600 ml) water with the milk, the sugar and the almond essence. Stir until the sugar is dissolved, and then stir in the dissolved gelatine. Pour into the cake tin, leave to cool and then chill in the fridge until set.

Meanwhile strain the juice from the tins of lychees into a saucepan and add the sugar and lemon juice. Put over the heat, stir until the sugar is dissolved, then bring to the boil and boil fiercely without stirring for 5 minutes.

When the almond mixture is set loosen the edges with a sharp knife and cut the jelly into 1-inch (2.5 cm) squares. Turn out carefully into a pretty glass bowl, arranging some of the squares up the sides of the bowl to make a depression in the middle. Shortly before serving spoon the lychees into the middle and spoon the syrup over them. Keep in the fridge until ready to serve.

Almond Dreams with Lychees, Casablanca Cakes

The Author

Josceline Dimbleby was born in Oxford in 1943. From the age of five her childhood was spent abroad, mostly in the Middle East and South America, so that at an early age she learned to appreciate a wide variety of food. She has travelled extensively in India, where she gained the experience of Indian cooking which inspired many of the recipes in this book.

Josceline's instinct has always been to create her own recipes, which results in varied and interesting dishes, but leading a very busy life herself she appreciates the value of advance preparation and simple methods and most of her recipes reflect this view without its affecting their originality in any way.

She has written many cookery articles for the national press and has featured on television and radio. Her first cookery book, *A Taste of Dreams*, appeared in 1976. This has now been reissued as a companion volume to her new book *Puddings, Desserts and Savouries*, which won the André Simon Award for the best cookery book of 1979. *Curries and Oriental Cookery* is the fourth in her series of cookbooks for Sainsbury's, following *Cooking for Christmas*, *Family Meat and Fish Cookery* and *Cooking with Herbs and Spices*.

Josceline lives in London with her husband, journalist and broadcaster David Dimbleby, and their three children.